50 Techniques Used in Co'

A Resource for Designers of Contemp

First Published in E
Author: Gill Mc
Designs by: Gill McGregor
Copyright © Gill McGregor 2014
Published by: Gill McGregor College
ISBN 978-0-9929332-0-3
Printed in the UK
Layout design: www.sosbusyweb.co.uk

Trademarks.
All trademarks are acknowledged as belonging to their respective companies.

Limit of Liability and Disclaimer of Warranty.
Whilst every effort has been made to make this book as accurate and complete as possible, the Publisher, the Author or anyone else involved with the preparation of this book accept no liability for the use of the techniques and materials, nor for errors or omissions, or changes that may subsequently be made.

Gill McGregor

As a Floral designer, Floristry and Flower Arrangement Teacher and NAFAS Demonstrator, I love to explore, experiment and develop ways of creating innovative and exciting designs using specific techniques, 'self made' containers and structures and of course all the wonderful products nature and manufacturers provide us.

To see my students, my clients and audiences enthuse and use the ideas and designs I teach and demonstrate fills me with joy, satisfaction and pride.

This book is designed to assist the selection process of Contemporary techniques to enhance your Floral designs.

With so many beautiful flowers, foliage and stems available – we have the enviable opportunity to further develop their natural beauty in order to create designs with greater impact. By using and arranging plant materials in an unusual way helps to create distinction: we can manipulate, cut, paint, wire, glue or arrange individual or group elements within a floral design to create the "wow" factor. Some techniques are easier to complete than others, some may be permanent and some only for the adventurous.

I have truly enjoyed producing this book and hope that you will find it a useful resource to further develop your Floral design skills.

Banding

Banding - the binding of a pliable material in close, neat order, to enhance or decorate. Wool, wire and grasses can be used. Banding can provide additional security or aesthetic enhancement.

The domed Carnation structures bound and banded with wool are arranged with rings banded with wool, sisal and raffia for effect and unity.

Basing

Basing - blocking, bedding and massing are all terms to describe the use of placing materials in close order to cover a foundation normally of a specific outline shape. Flowers, foliage or stems can be used, which can be flat, layered or domed. The key to success is to ensure the based material is neat, level and with no evident spaces showing unless desired. Materials used are often graded in size to assist the overall based visual effect.

The arrangement of Washingtonia robusta (Mexican fan palm) leaves encases a sculptured "eye" shaped wet foam foundation based with lemon Tulips.

This cushion is based with pinned Equisetum hyemale (Snake Grass) stems to create a "veined pattern". A spray of green Cymbidium Orchids completes this formal tribute.

Binding

Binding - the use of a pliable material to secure materials into position. The binding point must not travel. Wire, string, raffia or cable ties can be used.

This Calla lily down shower bouquet is constructed from precision cut Calla stems mounted onto wires which are then taped and brought through a wire binding point to secure and create a wire handle.

This spiralled stem hand tied uses string to bind all the materials into position.

Paper covered wire has been used to bind willow sticks for effect onto a taped flat ring.

Bunching / bundling
- the gathering of materials into bunches for effect with spiralling or parallel stems, secured with one or more binding points.

This 'self made', sisal covered container supports a simple arrangement of green Cymbidium Orchids, and 2 bunches of wheat.

Cable tying

Cable tying - the use of cable ties as a means of binding/ securing materials into position.

The Bamboo vase supports a 'self made' structure of bamboo lengths and slim bamboo cross sections secured by cable ties to provide unity in this arrangement of red Anthuriums

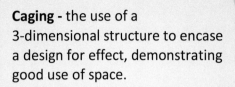

Caging - the use of a
3-dimensional structure to encase
a design for effect, demonstrating
good use of space.

This arrangement of
domed red Carnations is
caged with green midelino
sticks for effect.

Clamping

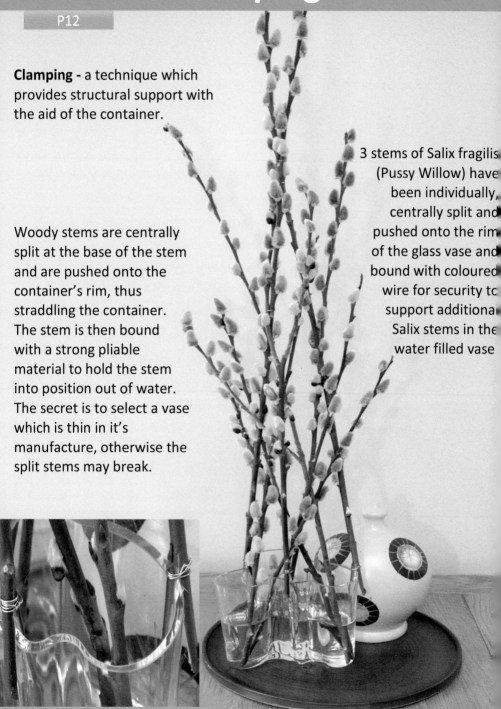

Clamping - a technique which provides structural support with the aid of the container.

Woody stems are centrally split at the base of the stem and are pushed onto the container's rim, thus straddling the container. The stem is then bound with a strong pliable material to hold the stem into position out of water. The secret is to select a vase which is thin in it's manufacture, otherwise the split stems may break.

3 stems of Salix fragilis (Pussy Willow) have been individually, centrally split and pushed onto the rim of the glass vase and bound with coloured wire for security to support additional Salix stems in the water filled vase

Clustering - thin stemmed materials are grouped together to form a small complete bunch, wired or not wired, and are inserted into the wet foam as if a single stem or as a wired cluster.

This 'self made' wood band container contains clusters of Alchemilla mollis and Bupleurum griffithii to enhance the Roses.

Cupping

Cupping - the manipulation of a flat leaf into a conical shape for effect, secured by wire, staples or glue.

This layered foliage design contains a base layer of cupped yellow variegated Hedera helix (Ivy) to help create the profile.

Cutting

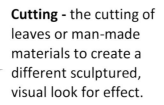

Cutting - the cutting of leaves or man-made materials to create a different sculptured, visual look for effect.

The arrangement of blue Agapanthus uses cut, sculptured Dypsis lutescens (Yellow Cane Palm), Fatsia japonica (Castor Oil) and Curcuma leaves.

Doming

Doming/pillowing - basing materials are positioned in close order to create a neat, level domed effect.

The circular medium has been based with cerise Carnations, framed with Rhapis excelsa (Finger Palm) and Cordyline fruticosa leaves and caged with Xanthorrhoea australis (Steel Grass) to provide enclosed space.

Drilling

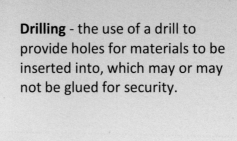

Drilling - the use of a drill to provide holes for materials to be inserted into, which may or may not be glued for security.

This 'self made' container was constructed using a spray painted cheese board with 6 drilled holes to house strong wires to aerially support the cylindrical container of willow, birch and a plastic liner.

Drying

Drying - the means of preserving plant material natural or manipulated for use in it's colour changed form or as spray painted for effect. Materials can be air dried, water dried or coated with one part PVA and one part water, before drying.

Plaited and woven Palms, manipulated Snake Grass structures (PVA protected), Pandanus and woven Phormium flowers are incorporated in this design
- a collection of previously used manipulated and cut foliage now dried and box stored in a dry place.

Edging

Edging - natural or manufactured material is attached or arranged to enhance the outline edge of a foundation. The edging material also protects the design within.

The posy pad has been edged with Prunus laurocerasus (Laurel).

The based heart and cushion are edged with single and double box pleated ribbon.

Feathering

Feathering - a technique which requires petals to be removed from a multiple petalled flower which are wired together to create a small petalled form, normally used in bridal work.

This Bridal design is constructed from 10 Carnations, 9 of which have been feathered into 5 petalled forms with the central Carnation surrounded by a card collar rather than it's calyx.

Folding

Folding/bending - stems and leaves can be bent and or folded to form an alternative shape secured either by the folded design or by wire, staples or glue.

A bouquet of folded Pandanus leaves is framed by an Arum italicum "pictum" leaf for effect. These "roses" can be air dried for further use.

Xanthorrhoea australis (Steel Grass) is bent to create angular and triangular shapes to enhance the designs of white Iris and Dracaena "Green tie".

Framing

Framing- the use of materials, natural or sculptured to provide a 2-dimensional frame around the focal area for enhancement. The frame can be partial or complete.

This minimalistic design relies upon the framing of the Pandanus leaves to emphasis the central white Gerbera and Salix fragilis (Pussy Willow) stems.

The wound Pandanus veitchii (Screw pine) leaves partially frame the design of yellow Roses.

Gluing

Gluing - the use of an adhesive in the construction of a design or component to secure or attach.

This 'self made' heart shaped, sculptured wire bridal design is completed with a Phalaenopsis Orchid attached with cool hot glue.

This 'self made' sisal sheet used to decorate a glass vase is made from PVA glue, sisal and wool.

Graduating

Graduating - when arranging a line of like materials and colour be it horizontal, curved, diagonal or vertical the flowers, foliage or accessories are graded in size. The smallest are positioned towards the outside of the design with the larger being positioned in graduated order towards the centre/ focal area.

Grouping

Grouping – to create greater impact like materials are grouped together in close order to form clusters. Arranging contrasting groups of different forms, textures and colours next to each other further enhances the design.

This design consists of groups or orange Roses,Picea pungens (Blue Pine) , Ilex (Holly), Cones and hips.

White Calla lilies are graduated to enhance this Xanthorrhoea australis (Steel Grass) woven screen.

Hedging

Hedging - is the positioning of plant material to mimic the look of a hedge, which can act as a screen, boundary or backdrop.

This wood and Sunflower design uses Chamaecyparis lawsoniana (Cupressus) to form a hedged screen to accentuate the Eucalyptus bark.

Interconnecting/Joining - the linking of 2 designs together using natural or man-made materials.

This design of pink Germinis uses bleached twigs to link the designs together for effect.

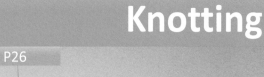

Knotting

Knotting - the tying of materials natural or man-made to produce a knot like structure.

A frill of looped and knotted Liriope gigantea (Lily Grass) edge this wired bridal Tulip posy.

Knotted Ficinea fascicularis (Flexigrass) is used to create a structure of enclosed space and to frame the Pandanus veitchii (Screw Pine) leaf.

Laminating

Laminating - materials are sealed within a heat sealed plastic pouch for effect, security or preservation.

This design evidences laminated sheets of coloured wool to decorate the glass vase and be incorporated as graduated discs within the design for unity.

Layering

Layering - the positioning of materials in layers for effect or to cover a foundation.
This technique is a form of basing.
Materials can be positioned to form decorative patterns e.g. Fleur de lis and are secured in neat, close order with pins or glue.

The layered Fleur de lis pattern of Prunus laurocerasus (Laurel) and Senecio greyii bases the extremities of this foliage "Hogarth Curve" design.

Looping

Looping - the securing of
natural or man-made materials
to form a loop/ loops.

This simple Leucospermum design evidences
looped Cordyline fruticosa "Kiwi" leaves together
with looped Dracaena marginata (Dragon tree) and
Liriope gigantea (Lily Grass).

Mossing

Mossing - the use of moss secured to a framework to provide a foundation or used as a decorative feature.

Both the Teddy and the wreath have been mossed with Tillandsia usneoides (Spanish moss).

Pinning

Pinning - the use of pins, with or without decorative heads, to secure materials into position.

A pattern of overlapping Prunus laurocerasus (Laurel) leaves are pinned against wet foam with decorative pins to form an oblong "living" vase.

This "living" vase of Liriope gigantea (Lily grass) and Liriope muscari (China grass) blades are inserted into the base of a wet foam sphere are secured into position in the well of the vase by steel dress making pins.

Pipping - the removal of individual florets from a multi headed flower which are used individually or as floret groups or strands, either glued or wired for security, mainly used in wedding designs.

These posy designs are constructed from individually wired florets of the sweet smelling Tuberose bound together to form domed Bridesmaid posies.

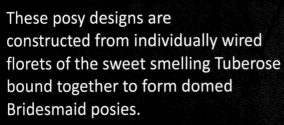

Gill McGregor College Publishers

Intensive courses focused on learning practical skills

Books, Courses and Workshops for Floristry, Flower Arranging, Professional and Traditional Crafts

Gill McGregor College Publishers 452 Goffs Lane, Goffs Oak, Hertfordshire, EN7 5EN

Tel: 01707 873944

www.gillmcgregorcollege.com

With Compliments

McGregor College Preparatory

Plaiting

Plaiting - a manipulation technique using natural or man-made flexible materials to create a decorative braid using 3 or more strands or groups of strands.

Both table arrangements have plaited Dypsis lutescens (Yellow Cane palm) leaves to provide enclosed space as a feature.

Pleating

Pleating - the folding and securing of natural or man-made materials to create a "ruffled" effect of uniform or random folds secured with staples, pins, glue, stitches or wires. Pleated ribbon: knife pleats and box pleats are a form of edging often used in Funeral work.

Random pleats of Aspidistra elatior (Cast Iron plant) secured with staples create the outline shape of this tasteful Cymbidium orchid arrangement.

Triple box pleated ribbon with mitred points in the colours of the Irish flag have been used to edge this Shamrock emblem funeral design.

Radiating

Radiating - The positioning of materials to radiate out from a focal area/ point of interest.

The elegant stems of the Singapore orchids radiate out from the centre of this free standing design.

Sculpturing

Sculpturing - the manipulation or carving of natural or man-made materials to create an alternative shape, which may require securing into position with a pliable material.

Asparagus virgatus (Tree Fern) has been bound together with coloured wire to create these 3- dimensional "horn-like" forms to frame the orange focal Roses.

Shadowing

Shadowing - the positioning of a second placement of similar material in shape /form to the side or back of the first placement to create a "shadow", thus providing depth within the design.

This design evidences the shadowing technique with the placements of sculptured Asparagus virgatus (Tree Fern), Pandanus, Philodendron xanadu (Fiddle Leaf) and Strelitzia reginae (Bird-of-paradise) leaves.

Sheltering

Sheltering - the use of a structure or plant material which when positioned provides an "umbrella" sheltered effect over the design, thus providing greater emphasis on space.

The Philodendron xanadu (Fiddle Leaf) leaves provide the shelter over this arrangement of pink Germinis and Equisetum hyemale (Snake Grass) discs.

Spiralling

Spiralling - the placement of materials/ stems at a constant diagonal angle so they splay out and thus evidence a spiralled effect. The stems are normally bound together with a pliable material: string, wire or a cable tie. The binding point must not travel.

The Equisetum hyemale (Snake Grass) stems are internally support wired and were bent and secured into graduated sized triangular shapes. This 3-dimensional structure is constructed by pinning the triangles together to form a spiral.

The stems of this hand tied have been spiralled and bound with string to secure the materials into position.

Spray Painting

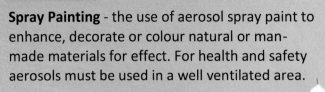

Spray Painting - the use of aerosol spray paint to enhance, decorate or colour natural or man-made materials for effect. For health and safety aerosols must be used in a well ventilated area.

An Arachniodes adiantiformis (Leather) leaf has been placed over Strelitzia reginae (Bird-of-Paradise) leaves and sprayed lightly with black and white spray paint to create this misty leaf silhouette pattern.

Fatsia japonica (Castor Oil) leaves were placed on this background and sprayed with 3 different paints whilst moving the Fatsias each time to create this ethereal background design.

Stacking

Stacking - the placement of materials or forms on top of each other securely to create a layered pile.

Squares of wet foam based with woven Pandanus leaves have been stacked by threading the squares at the corners onto an upturned pedestal top which is placed onto a dish and completed with a spray of red Anthuriums.

Stapling

Stapling - the means of a securing materials into position with a 'self made' or manufactured staple.

The coils of the Pandanus are secured into position by manufactured staples.

The pleated folds of the Aspidistra elatior (Cast Iron plant) leaves are secured with manufactured staples.

Stitching

Stitching — the use of a pliable material which is threaded through natural or man-made material to create a decorative pattern, to secure materials together or as a specific wiring method to support wire leaves.

The Hedera helix (Ivy) leaf is stitched one third down from the tip for support.

Sisal discs are stitched with wire onto a willow roll to create this 'self made' container.

Structure Constructing

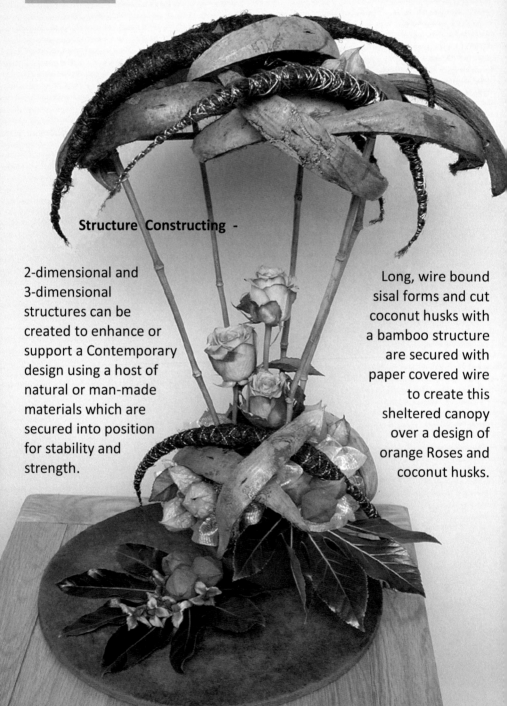

Structure Constructing -

2-dimensional and 3-dimensional structures can be created to enhance or support a Contemporary design using a host of natural or man-made materials which are secured into position for stability and strength.

Long, wire bound sisal forms and cut coconut husks with a bamboo structure are secured with paper covered wire to create this sheltered canopy over a design of orange Roses and coconut husks.

Terracing

Terracing - the layered placement of like materials to form a "stepped" formation with space between each placement. Materials are positioned to "zig zag" slightly from side to side for effect. Terracing is normally used to disguise the mechanics of a design.

This free standing design of Mango Calla lilies and Sunflowers evidences terraced placements of Fatsia japonica (Castor Oil) and Bergenia cordifolia (Elephants Ear) leaves.

Threading

Threading - natural or man-made materials are pierced and strung onto a pliable or rigid material to create a lei or string of materials to be worn or used for decorative purposes.

Black beads and drilled white painted twigs are threaded onto heavy gauge wires to enhance the arrangement of white Gerberas.

Carnations are threaded through the calyx with aluminium wire to create this Carnation ring.

Tubing

Tubing - the manipulation of leaves or man-made materials to form tubular shapes secured into position by binding, gluing, stapling or pinning.

Dracaena "Green tie" have been manipulated into tubes and secured with decorative pins to create the height of this blue Agapanthus design.

Veiling

Veiling - the use of a light material which is placed onto all or part of the design to create a translucent look.

Tillandsia usneoides (Spanish Moss)is placed on parts of the completed white Calla lily design to create a veiled, misty effect.

Waxing

Waxing - the use of wax as a mechanic, or as a decorative element or sealant.

The ends of 90 gauge wires have been heated with a flame and then inserted into used wax candles to create skewers of varying height. Dried Equisetum hyemale (Snake Grass) discs, dried Rhapis excelsa (Finger Palm) leaves and white Calla lilies with curved stems and sealed with wax are arranged on the skewers for effect.

Weaving

Weaving - natural or man-made materials are woven using the warp and weft method to make 2 or 3-dimensional shapes, to base a foundation, or if loosely woven, make a "rose-like" structure.

A woven disc made of willow sticks, Xerophyllum tenax (Bear Grass) and Xanthorrhoea australis (Steel Grass) provides the outline base of this Tulip arrangement.

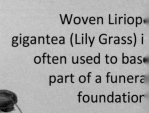

Woven Liriope gigantea (Lily Grass) i often used to base part of a funera foundation

Woven Pandanus veitchii (Screw Pine) is the "living" foundation for this simple square design.

Winding

Winding – natural or man-made materials are wound around itself, secured if necessary, to create an interesting manipulated form.

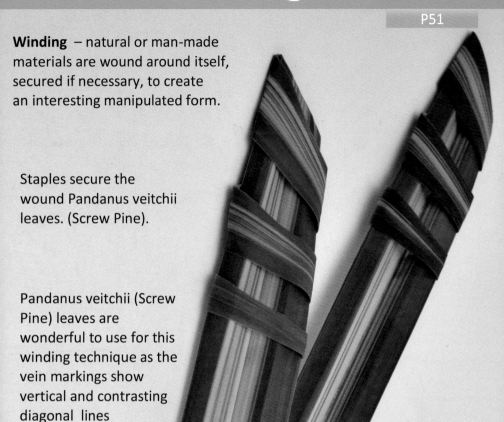

Staples secure the wound Pandanus veitchii leaves. (Screw Pine).

Pandanus veitchii (Screw Pine) leaves are wonderful to use for this winding technique as the vein markings show vertical and contrasting diagonal lines

as seen in this Contemporary orange Rose arrangement.

Wiring

Wiring - this technique uses different gauge wires according to their usage to: externally wire, semi- internally wire or internally wire materials for support, anchorage and control.

Equisetum hyemale (Snake grass) is internally wired to support the bent stems to create these simple lantern and Christmas tree designs.

There are a host of different wires available: binding wire, cut lengths of silver, green coated or blue annealed wire and decorative wires.

Wiring is used to help prevent breakage of heads from a stem or breakage of a stem itself.

Wiring is used to assist anchorage into a foundation or medium with the use of single or double leg mounts.

Wiring

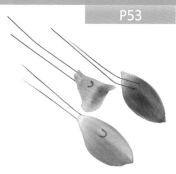

For bridal work the stems are often removed and replaced with a wire to make the design lighter and or to create a handle. Alternatively individual bracts, petals or florets are wired to construct a range of bridal items.

Wiring can also control the positioning of a material. An example of which is the stitched wiring method.

The bracts of the Curcuma are individually wired to create this composite bouquet edged with stitched Hedera helix (Ivy) leaves.

Taping

Taping - goes hand in hand with wiring. The use of a manufactured tape to cover wire and other materials for neatness.

Many wired items use tape to hide the binding point or to make the wires a different colour for aesthetic reasons.

Taping can hold light weight materials together.

The wired Phalaenopsis Orchid with a variety of wired and taped components makes up this elegant buttonhole.

Wrapping

Wrapping - the use of natural or man-made materials to externally encase, fully or partially, inner materials for effect, protection or additional security.

This purple Calla lily Bridal hand tied is wrapped with a manufactured wrap for effect